RECORDED VERSIONS
GUITAR

AUTHENTIC TRANSCRIPTIONS
WITH NOTES AND TABLATURE

BUDDY GUY

Damn Right, I've Got The Blues

T0051160

Cover photo by Herb Snitzer
Interior photos by Paul Natkin

ISBN 978-0-7935-1918-7

HAL•LEONARD®
CORPORATION

7777 W. BLUEMOUND RD. P.O. BOX 13819 MILWAUKEE, WI 53213

Visit Hal Leonard Online at
www.halleonard.com

CONTENTS

BUDDY GUY

Blues Blaster

Buddy Guy uses a rhythm section as a launching pad from which to hurtle his guitar into sonic orbit. And, while he sometimes follows the established trajectories charted by his predecessors, he regularly explores the outer reaches of harmony where no blues guitarist has gone before.

Born in Lettsworth, Louisiana in 1936, George "Buddy" Guy moved to Chicago in 1957. By 1960, with the help of Muddy Waters, he had built a reputation as a hired gun while waxing future classics like "The First Time I Met the Blues" under his own name. In addition, he haunted the jam sessions, cutting the head of every Windy City axeman who challenged him. At a time when master string chokers such as Freddie King, Otis Rush and Magic Sam prowled the Southside blues clubs, Buddy's furious fretboard forays and pleading vocals commanded attention.

The 1960s saw the beginning of his long association with Junior Wells. *Hoodoo Man Blues* (Delmark DS-612) and *It's My Life, Baby* (Vanguard VSD-79231) define the blues guitar trio as Buddy comps close voiced dominant chords, doubles bass lines and squeezes out prickly solos and fills behind Junior's plaintive vocals and succinct harp work.

In the late sixties, Vanguard Records issued three solo albums to wide critical acclaim. *This Is Buddy Guy* (VSD-79290), *Hold That Plane* (VSD-79323) and the landmark *A Man and the Blues* (VSD-79272) revealed a mature and confident virtuoso. In contrast to his small club band with Junior, here Buddy fronts a raucous big band, horns bleeding in sympathy as his urgent singing sets up his silky, out of phase Strat.

Commercial acceptance on the level of Jimi Hendrix – who was influenced by Buddy, as were Stevie Ray Vaughan, Eric Clapton, Jeff Beck and Jimmy Page – was predicted, but never materialized. Though audiences were thrilled with its wanton rave ups, the record companies did not get it. Buddy's recording career lay dormant in the 1970s and a potential guitar hero remained the blues community's secret weapon.

Finally, in 1981, two remarkable albums were released that represented the next evolutionary step in blues guitar. *Stone Crazy* (Alligator AL 4723) is almost frightening in its brutal intensity. "Sheets of sound", a term once applied to John Coltrane's saxophone onslaught, burst from tracks like "I Smell a Rat". This ten minute opus expresses the rage of a man who thinks he is being cheated on, manifesting itself in an incredibly vicious attack of flesh on strings. As with all of his best work, the dramatic use of dynamics, where his voice and guitar careen from a scream to a whisper, makes this cut awesome in its raw, emotional power.

Likewise, *D.J. Play My Blues* (JSP Records 1042) showcases blistering fretwork while highlighting Buddy's reverence for his mentors on the mellow "Dedication to T-Bone Walker". Also included in this varied set is the incendiary instrumental shuffle, "Just Teasin'". A virtual guitar lesson on tension and release, this tune propels Buddy to use wobbly slurs, severe over-bends, whiplash vibrato and crackling distortion in a dizzying roller coaster ride of a solo.

Stylistically, T-Bone Walker began the electric blues guitar era in the 1940s with his "modern arpeggio playing". B.B. King presented fluid string bending and vibrato in the 1950s. Albert King popularized the long, bent note sustain of the 1960s. Johnny Winter brought high octane Texas blues to arenas in the 1970s, while Buddy's "in your face" aural assault forecast the screaming virtuosity prevalent in rock and blues of the 1980s. But, despite the accolades of stars like Stevie Ray, the premier power blues guitarist remained without a major label recording until *Damn Right, I've Got the Blues* (Silvertone 1462-2-J) in 1991. After far too many years of music industry indifference, Buddy finally got his due with this hit blues album.

With a respectful nod to the late Willie Dixon, Buddy Guy is the blues. He has the passion, soul and courage to play what he feels, secure in the knowledge that his place in history is predicated on the love that he has for the blues tradition and the artists who inspired him.

Dave Rubin

Damn Right, I've Got the Blues

By Buddy Guy

You're

End Rhy. Fig. 1

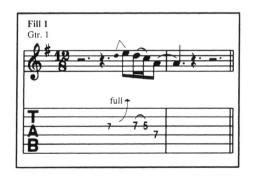

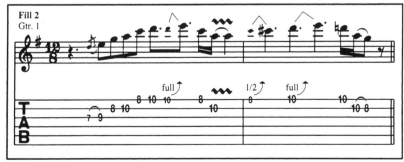

'cause I don't have a thing . to lose.
to the door and said, "Grand-dad-dy,   you   know   ain't   no one at home."

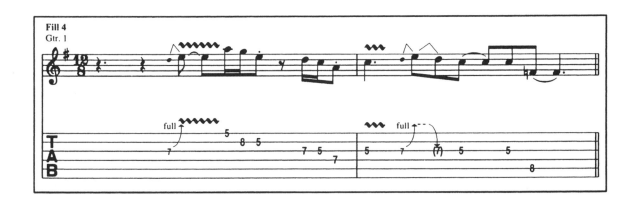

Gtr. 2: w/ Rhy. Fig. 1 simile

Guitar Solo

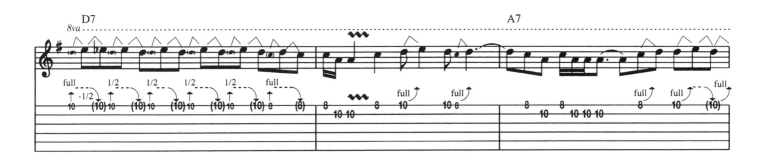

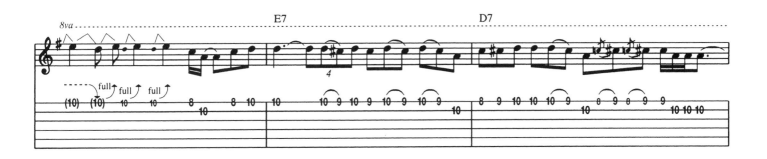

You're

⊕ *Coda*

Gtr. 2: Cont. w/ Fill 7

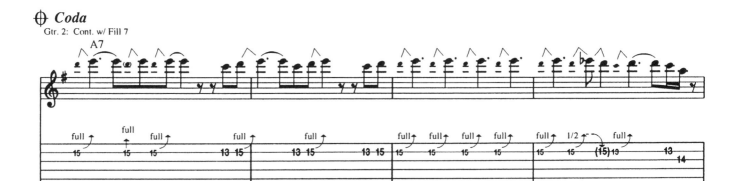

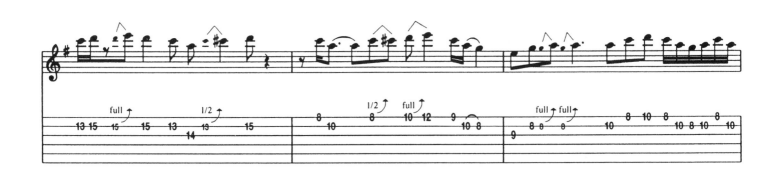

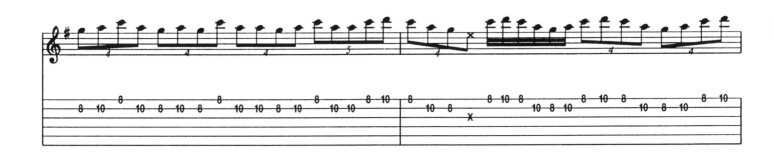

Fill 7
Gtr. 2

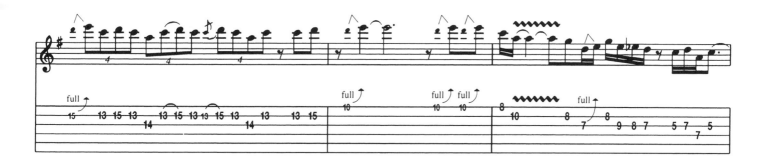

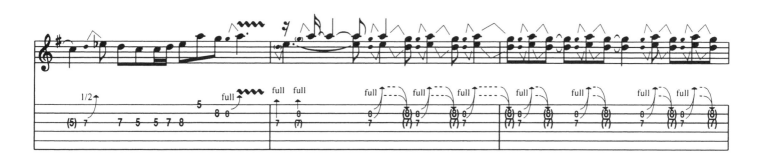

Gtr. 2: w/ Fill 7 to end

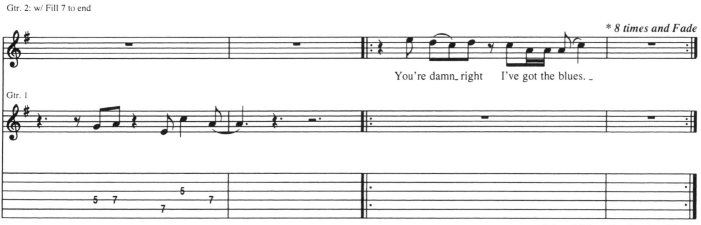

You're damn right   I've got the blues.

Gtrs. 1 & 2 continue in unison 5th time

Where Is the Next One Coming From

By John Hiatt

Where? ___ Oh, where ___ huh, where is the next one com-in' from? ___
(Where?)

Fill 5
Gtr. 2

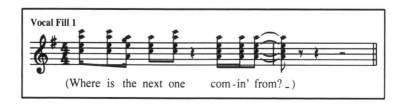

Vocal Fill 1

(Where is the next one com-in' from? _)

Where is the next one com-in' from? ___

Bridge

I want more, _____ oo-oh - wo - oo-oh. Gim-me. Gim-me. Gim-me. Gim-me.

Fill 3
Gtr. 3

slow gliss.

nat - u - ral thing _____ for an an - i - mal.

(Where is   the next one com-in' from? _)

Well I'm

tired   all ___ of that give and take. _____

(Where is   the next one com-in' from? _____)

A - bout

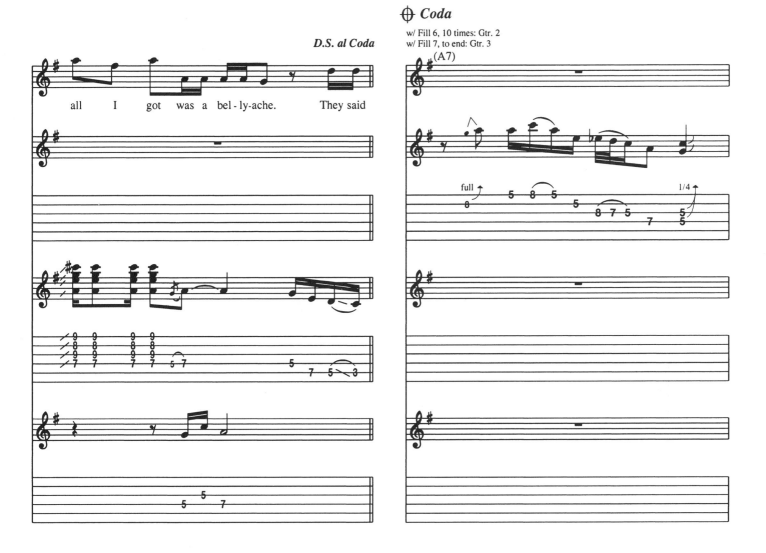

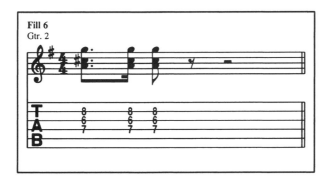

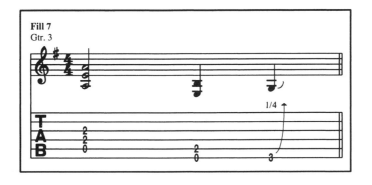

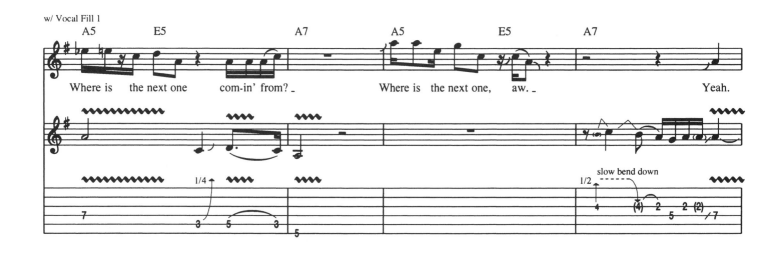

Where is the next one com-in' from? _ Where is the next one, aw. _ Yeah.

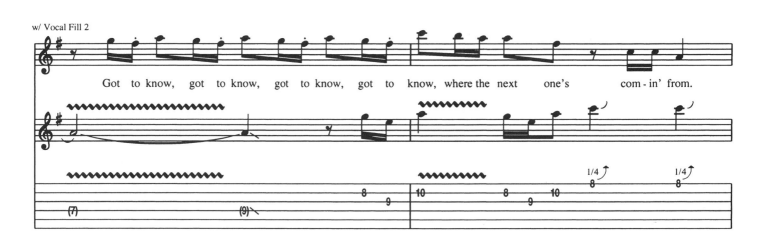

Got to know, got to know, got to know, got to know, where the next one's com-in' from.

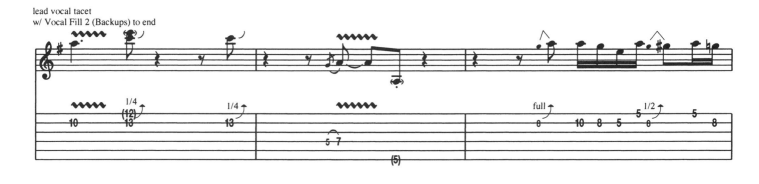

lead vocal tacet
w/ Vocal Fill 2 (Backups) to end

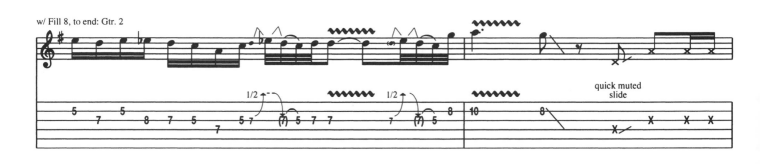

w/ Fill 8, to end: Gtr. 2

Vocal Fill 2

(Where is the next one com-in' from?)

Five Long Years

Words and Music by Eddie Boyd

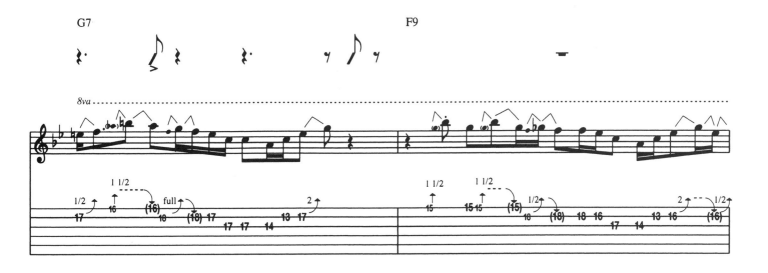

Yes, have you ev-er been mis-treat-ed? _____   Then you got to,   a you

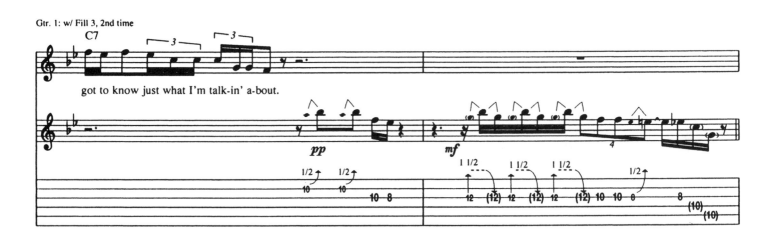

Gtr. 1: w/ Fill 3, 2nd time

got to know just what I'm talk-in' a-bout.

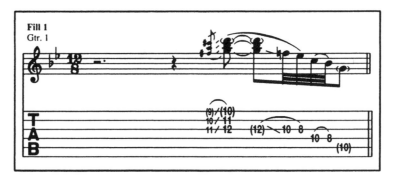

Fill 1
Gtr. 1

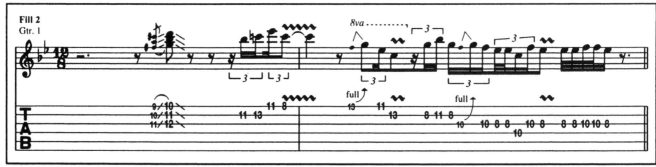

Fill 2
Gtr. 1

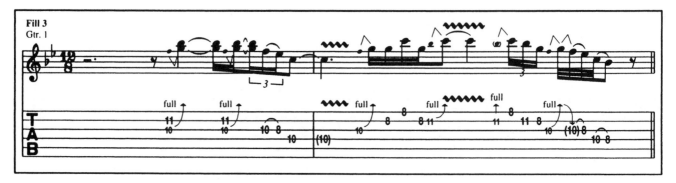

Fill 3
Gtr. 1

Mis-treat-ed, _ then you got to, you've got to know just what I'm talk-in' a-bout.

Lord, I work five long years for one wom-an, _ and she had the nerve _____

to kick me out. _ Lord, but I fin-'ly learned a les-son,

Fill 5
Gtr. 1

Fill 3
Gtr. 1

Fill 9
Gtr. 1

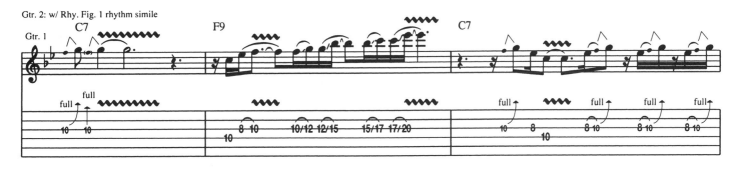

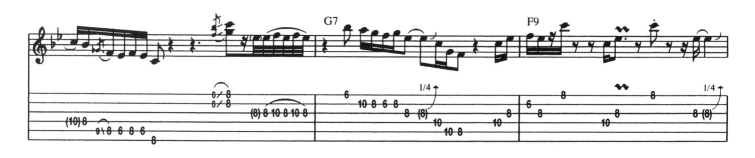

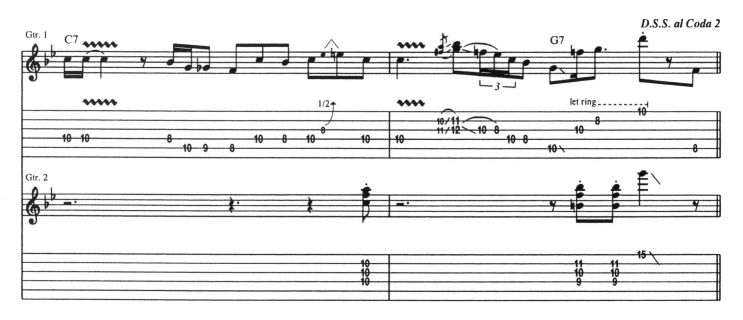

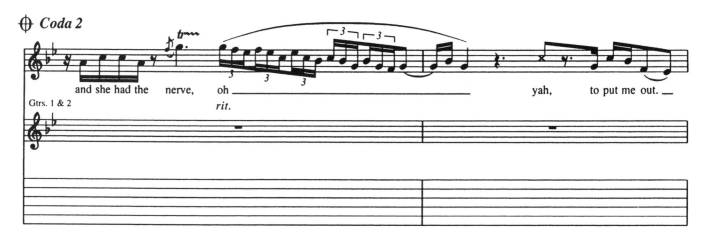

and she had the nerve, oh _____ yah, to put me out. ___

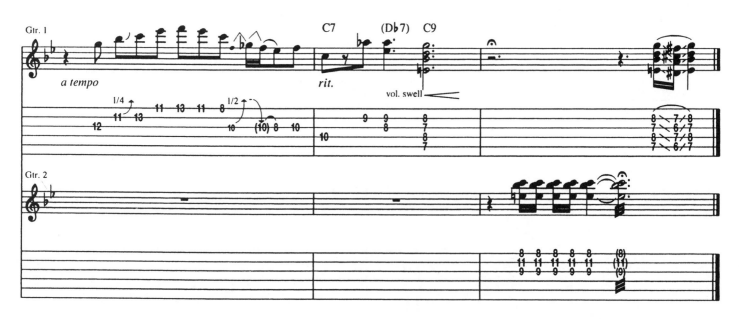

Mustang Sally

Words and Music by Bonny Rice

slow your Mus-tang down.   Now you're go-in' a-round sig-ni-fy-in' wom-an,   you don't wan-na let me ride.

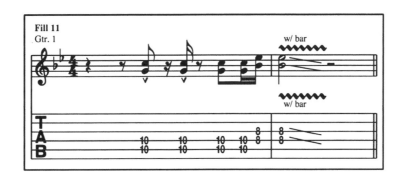

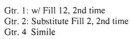

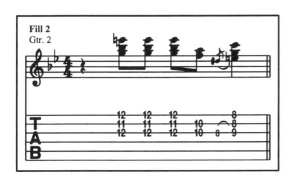

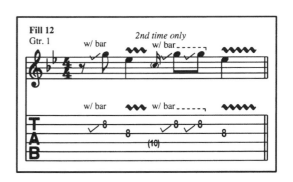

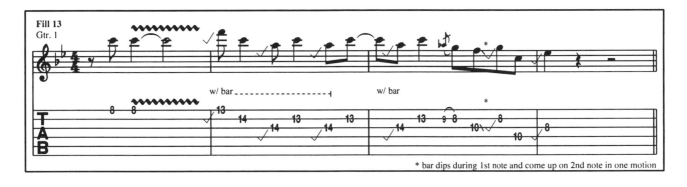

* bar dips during 1st note and come up on 2nd note in one motion

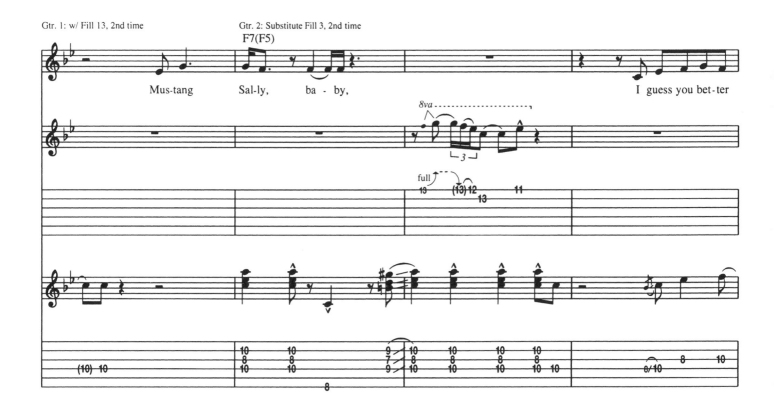

Gtr. 1: w/ Fill 13, 2nd time

Gtr. 2: Substitute Fill 3, 2nd time

F7(F5)

Mus-tang   Sal-ly,   ba - by,   I guess you bet-ter

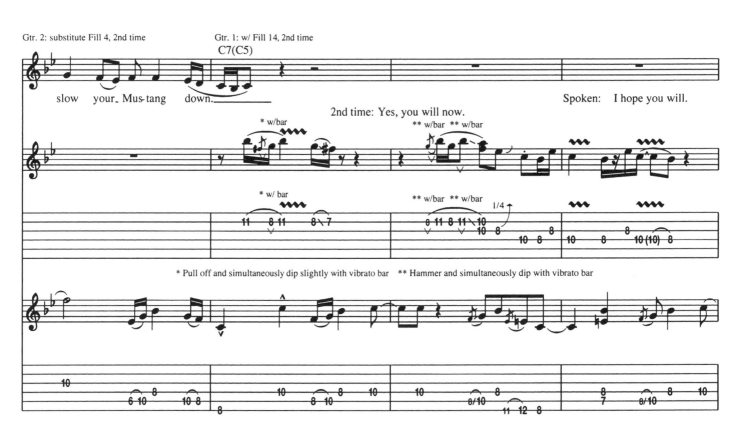

Gtr. 2: substitute Fill 4, 2nd time

Gtr. 1: w/ Fill 14, 2nd time

C7(C5)

slow   your Mus-tang   down.

2nd time: Yes, you will now.   Spoken: I hope you will.

* Pull off and simultaneously dip slightly with vibrato bar   ** Hammer and simultaneously dip with vibrato bar

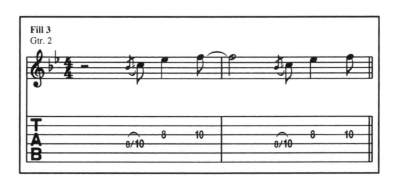

Fill 3
Gtr. 2

You bet-ter run it all __ o-ver town. __

Gon-na run all o-ver town. __

I guess I bet-ter

I'm gon-na put your

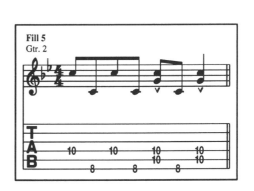

Fill 4
Gtr. 2

Fill 5
Gtr. 2

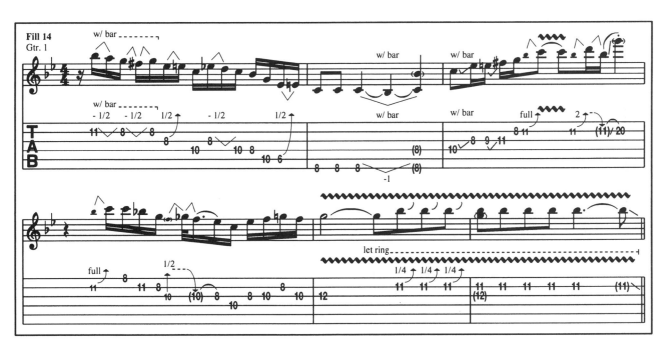

Fill 14
Gtr. 1

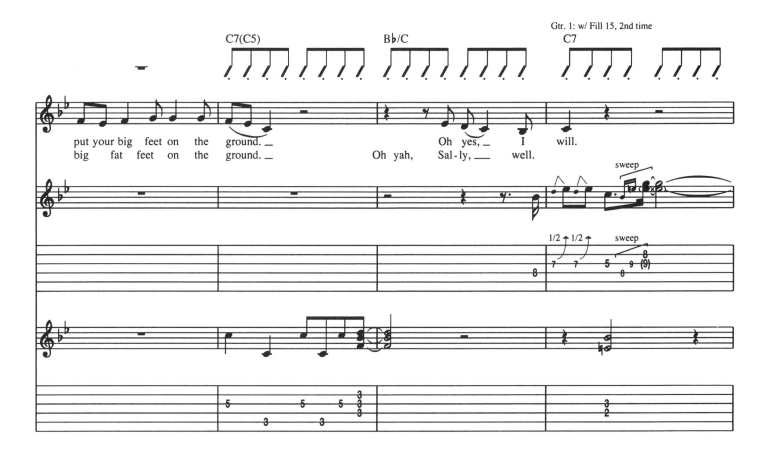

put your big feet on the ground. ___ Oh yes, ___ I will.
big fat feet on the ground. ___ Oh yah, Sal-ly, ___ well.

All you wan-na do is ride ___ a-round Sal-ly.

Backups: (Ride Sal-ly, ride..

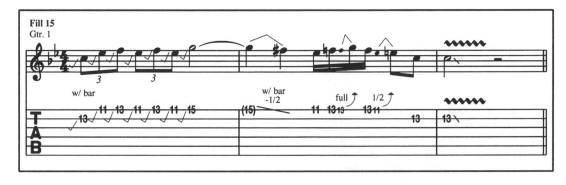

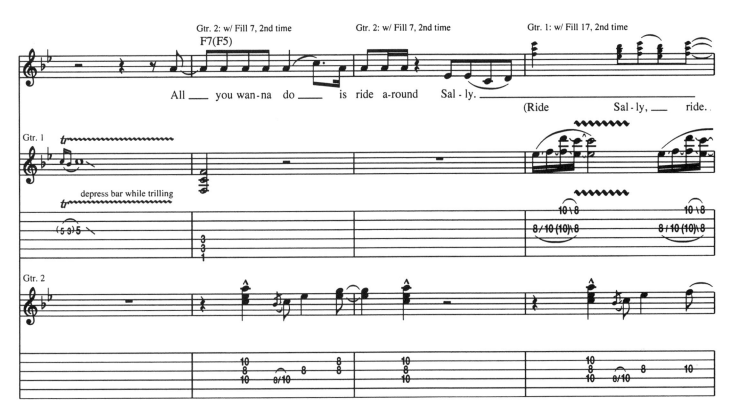

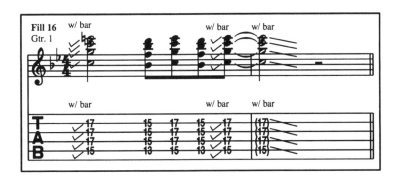

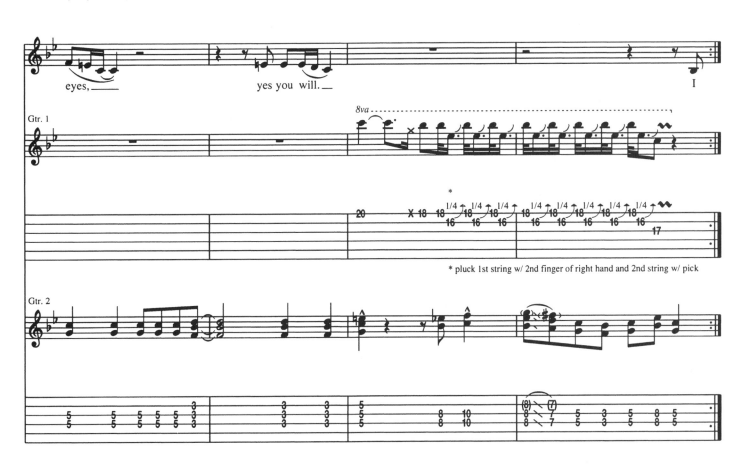

* pluck 1st string w/ 2nd finger of right hand and 2nd string w/ pick

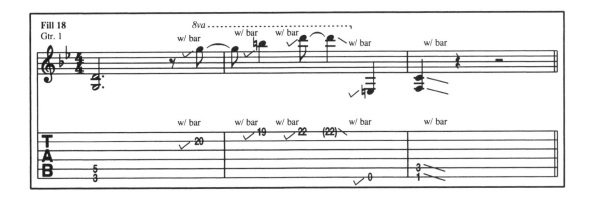

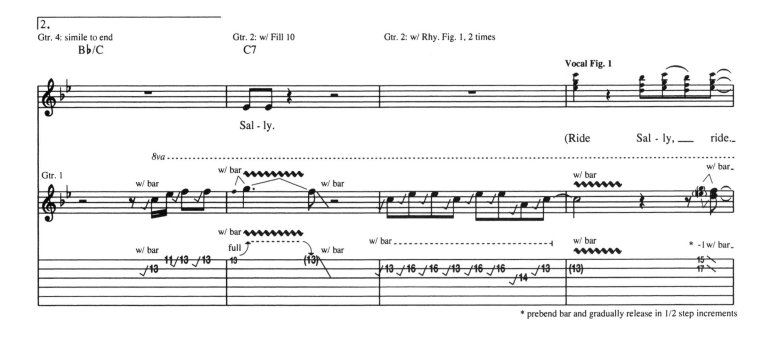

Gtr. 4: simile to end

Gtr. 2: w/ Fill 10

Gtr. 2: w/ Rhy. Fig. 1, 2 times

Bb/C

C7

Vocal Fig. 1

Sal - ly.

(Ride   Sal - ly, ___ ride.

Gtr. 1

* prebend bar and gradually release in 1/2 step increments

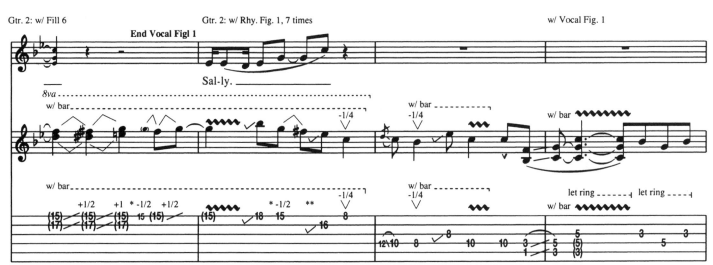

Gtr. 2: w/ Fill 6

Gtr. 2: w/ Rhy. Fig. 1, 7 times

w/ Vocal Fig. 1

End Vocal Fig1 1

Sal-ly.

* G is bent down 1/2 step w/ bar   ** bar is held down while picking the E, then released

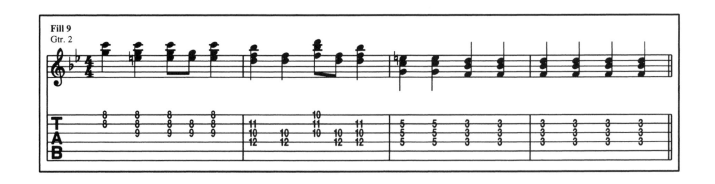

Fill 9
Gtr. 2

Fill 10
Gtr. 2

* depress bar while trilling

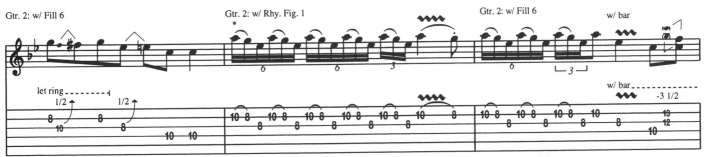

* pluck 2nd string w/ middle finger of right hand, pulloff, and pluck 3rd string w/ pick

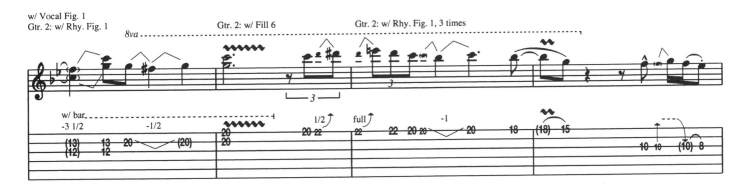

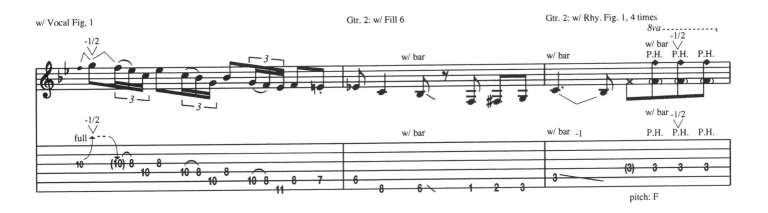

There Is Something on Your Mind

By Big Jay McNeely

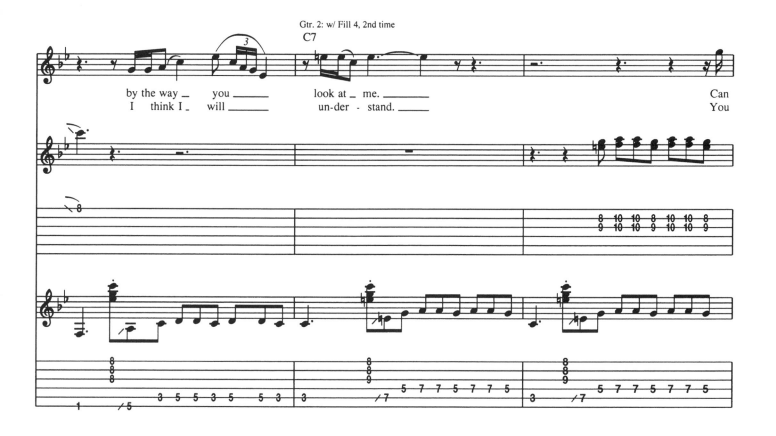

by the way __ you _____ look at __ me. _____ Can
I think I __ will _____ un-der - stand. _____ You

Fill 2
Gtr. 2

Fill 6
Gtr. 2

Fill 3
Gtr. 2

Fill 7
Gtr. 2

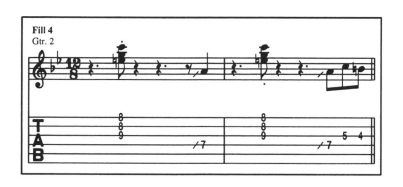

Fill 4
Gtr. 2

Additional Lyrics

Verse 3

If you ever think about me,
If I ever cross your mind,
Oh, if you ever think about me, baby,
If I ever cross your mind,
I want you to know, I want you to know
That you, you, you, you're mine.

Early in the Mornin'

Words and Music by Leo Hickman, Louis Jordan and Dallas Bartley

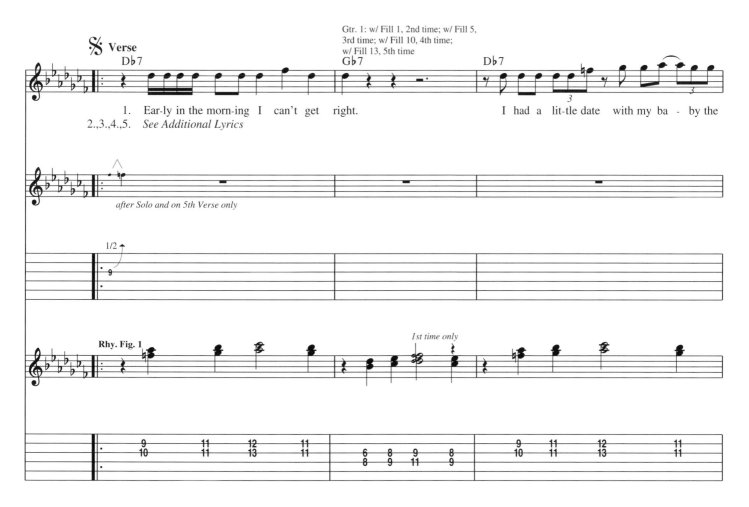

Gtr. 1: w/ Fill 1, 2nd time; w/ Fill 5,
3rd time; w/ Fill 10, 4th time;
w/ Fill 13, 5th time

1. Ear-ly in the morn-ing I can't get right.
2.,3.,4.,5. *See Additional Lyrics*

I had a lit-tle date with my ba - by the

after Solo and on 5th Verse only

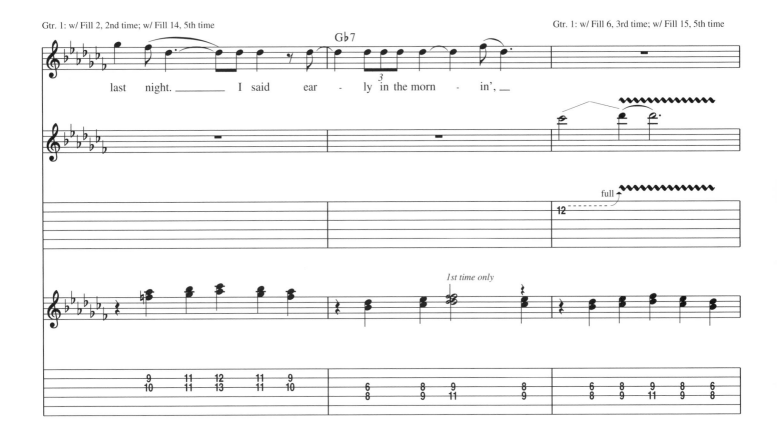

last night. _____ I said ear - ly in the morn - in', __

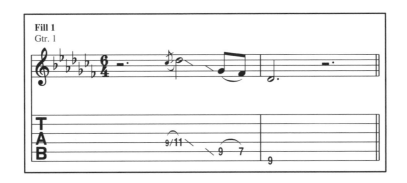

Fill 1
Gtr. 1

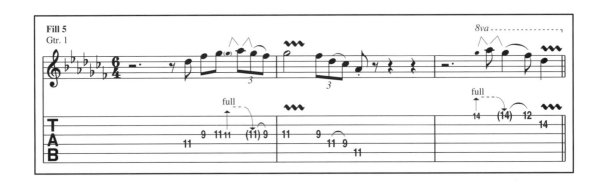

Fill 5
Gtr. 1

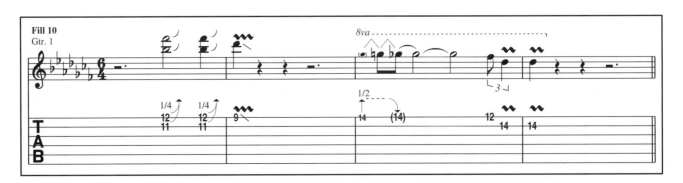

Fill 10
Gtr. 1

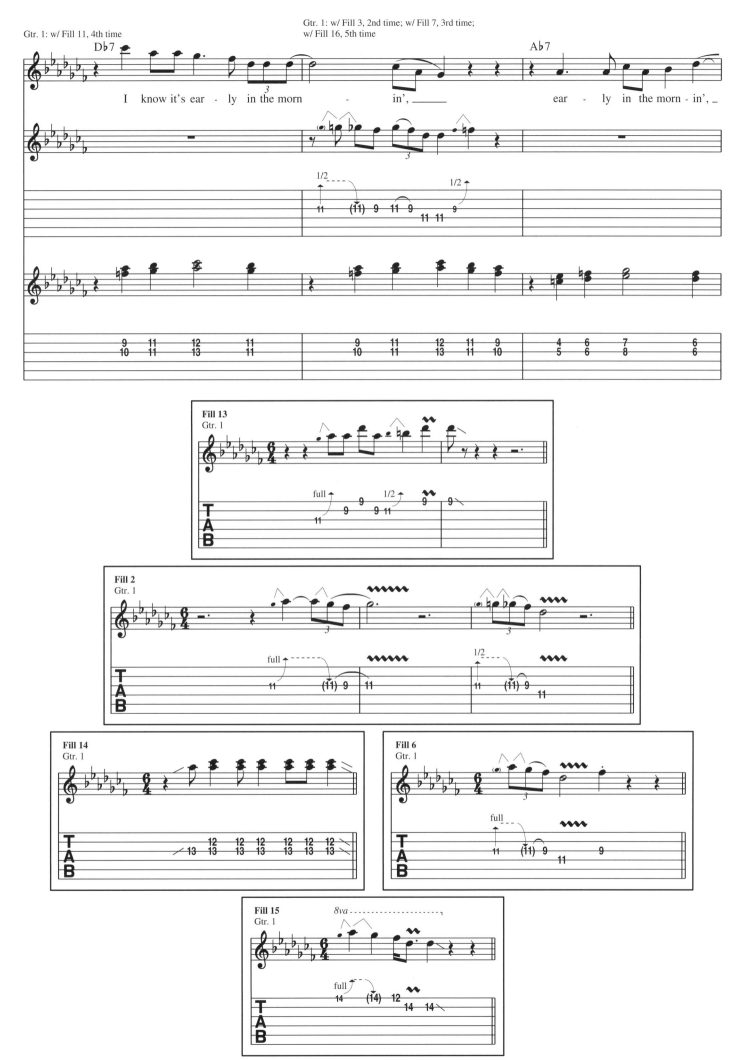

Gtr. 1: w/ Fill 4, 2nd time; w/ Fill 8, 3rd time

Gtr. 1: w/ Fill 9, 3rd time; w/ Fill 4, 4th time;
w/ Fill 17, 5th time

To Coda ⊕ | 1.,2.,3.

and I ain't got   noth-in' but the blues.

End Rhy. Fig. 1

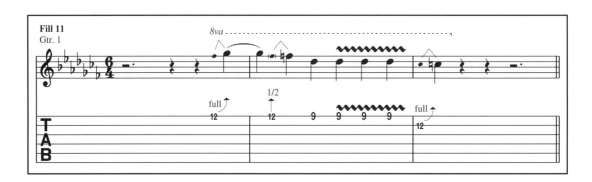

Fill 11
Gtr. 1

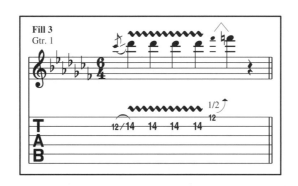

Fill 3
Gtr. 1

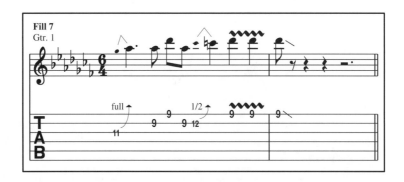

Fill 7
Gtr. 1

To Coda

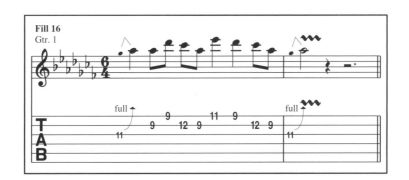

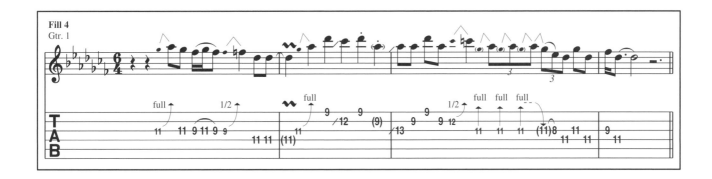

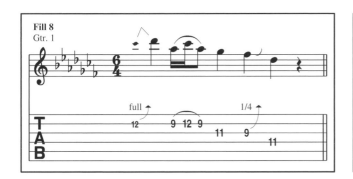

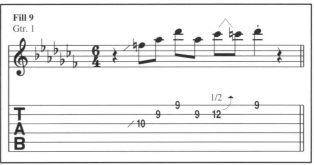

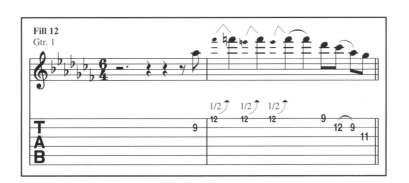

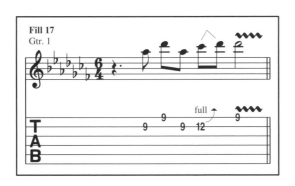

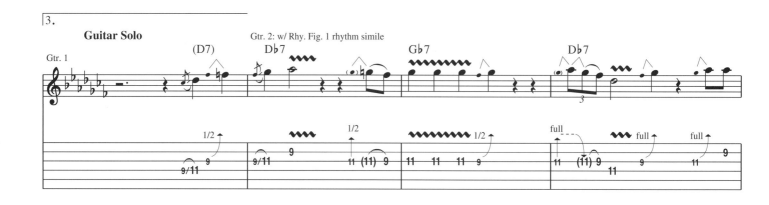

Guitar Solo

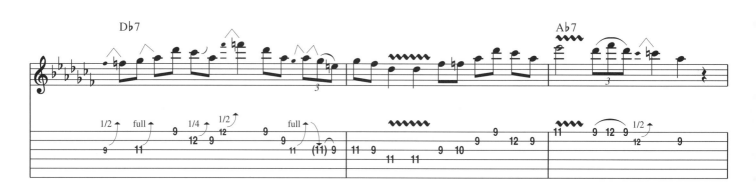

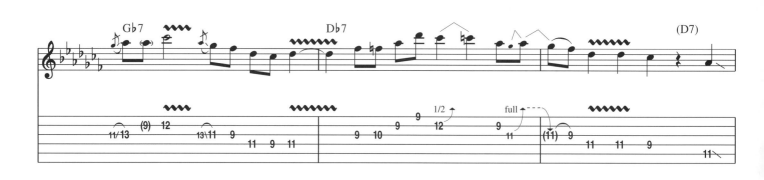

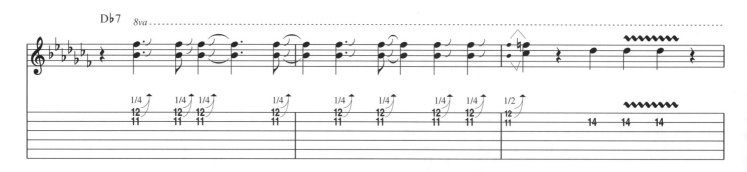

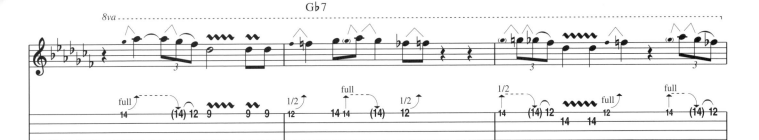

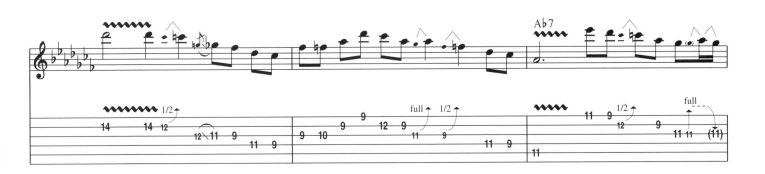

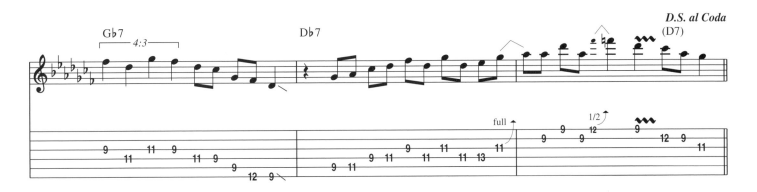

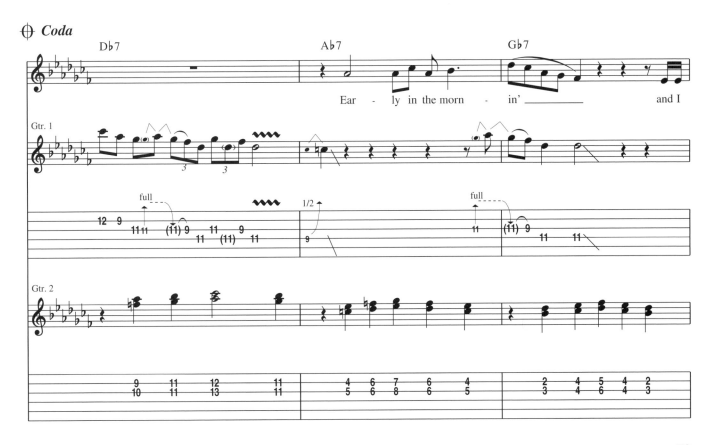

Ear - ly in the morn - in' _____ and I

ain't got noth-in' but the blues. _____

Additional Lyrics

Verse 2

I went to the place where we used to go.
I went to her house and she don't live there no more.

Verse 3

I went to a girlfriend's house and she was out.
I knocked on her father's door and he began to shout.

Verse 4

I went to ? to get me somethin' to eat.
The way she looked at me said, Buddy, you sure look beat.

Verse 5

I had a lot of money when I started out.
I can't ? my baby, you know my money will run out.

Too Broke to Spend the Night

By Buddy Guy

Gtr. 1: w/ Fill 2, 2nd time; w/ Fill 6, 3rd time; w/ Fill 11, 4th time

I know it ain't right.

am.
ring.

I said my
I said, yah I

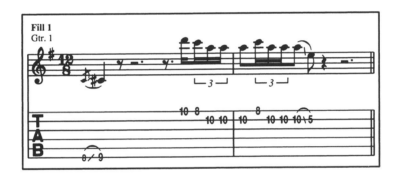

* G note is hit quasi-accidentally. Don't adjust your fingering.

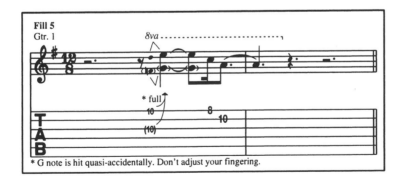

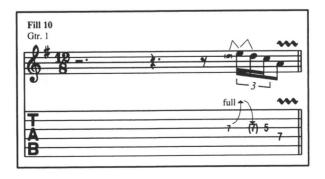

Gtr. 1: w/ Fill 7, 3rd time

Gtr. 1: w/ Fill 12, 4th time

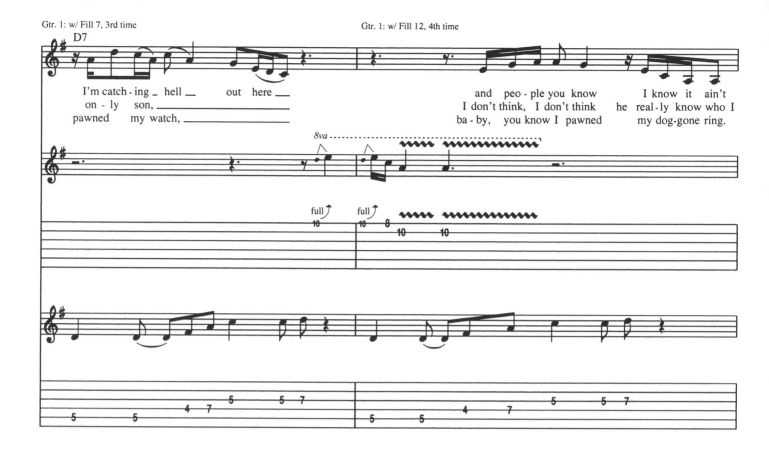

I'm catch-ing _ hell _ out here _
on - ly son, _____
pawned my watch, _____

and peo - ple you know
I don't think, I don't think
ba - by, you know I pawned

I know it ain't
he real-ly know who I
my dog-gone ring.

Fill 2
Gtr. 1

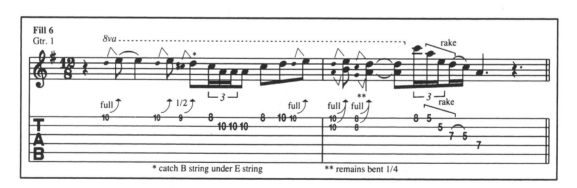

Fill 6
Gtr. 1

* catch B string under E string

** remains bent 1/4

Fill 11
Gtr. 1

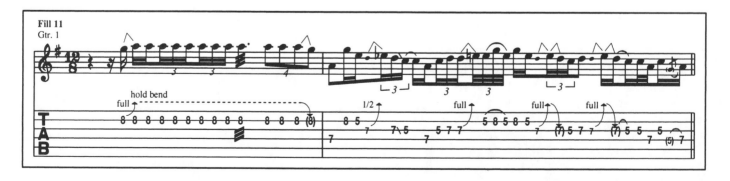

Gtr. 1: w/ Fill 3, 2nd time

'Cause I'm so broke, I'm so broke right now, ___   that I can't e - ven spend the
Frank - ly speak-ing peo-ple, ___   I don't think, I don't think he real - ly gives a
You know I'm try - in' to ride this old rack - e - ty bike   and I don't e - ven have a dog - gone

Gtr. 1: w/ Fill 4, 2nd time; w/ Fill 9, 3rd time; w/ Fill 14, 4th time

To Coda ⊕

End Rhy. Fig. 1

night.
damn.
chain.

Fill 13
Gtr. 1

Fill 3
Gtr. 1

Gtr. 2: w/ Rhy. Fig. 1

Guitar Solo

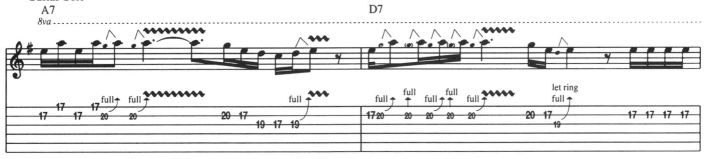

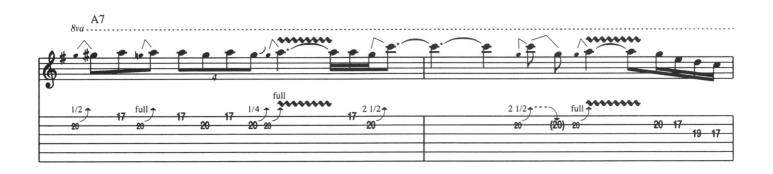

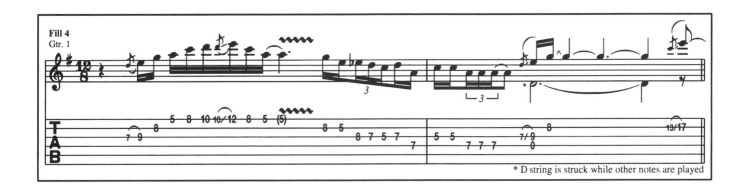

* D string is struck while other notes are played

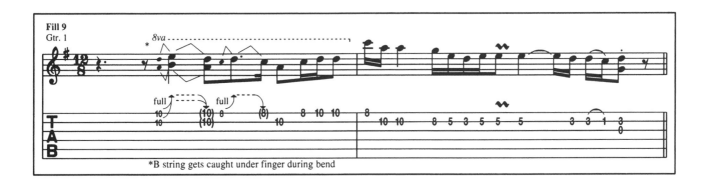

*B string gets caught under finger during bend

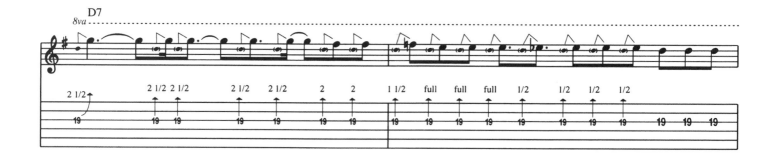

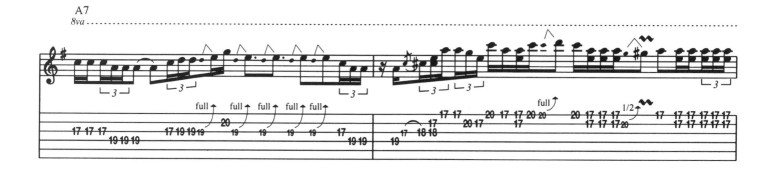

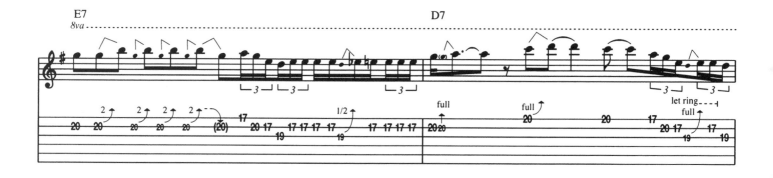

D.S. al Coda

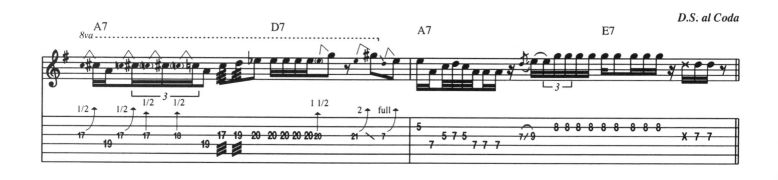

Coda

Gtr. 2: w/ Rhy. Fig. 1, Bars 1 - 10

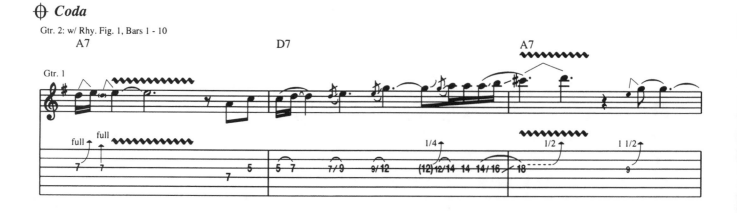

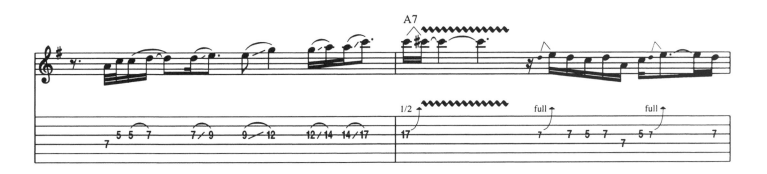

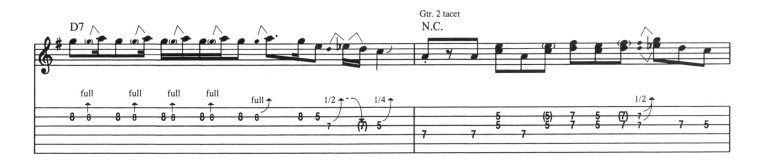

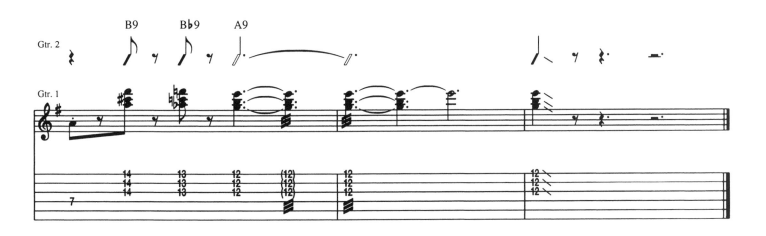

Black Night

Words and Music by Jessie Mae Robinson

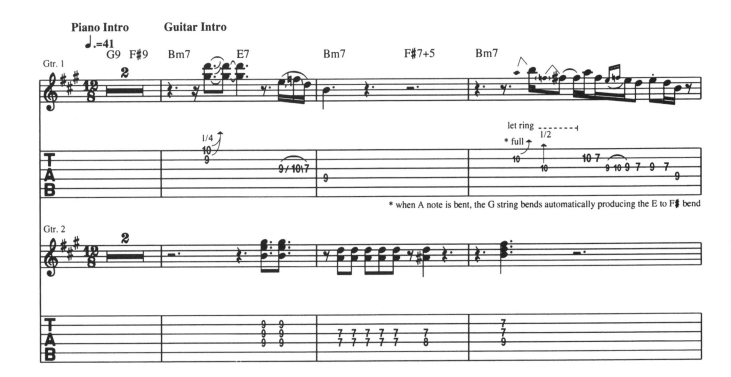

* when A note is bent, the G string bends automatically producing the E to F♯ bend

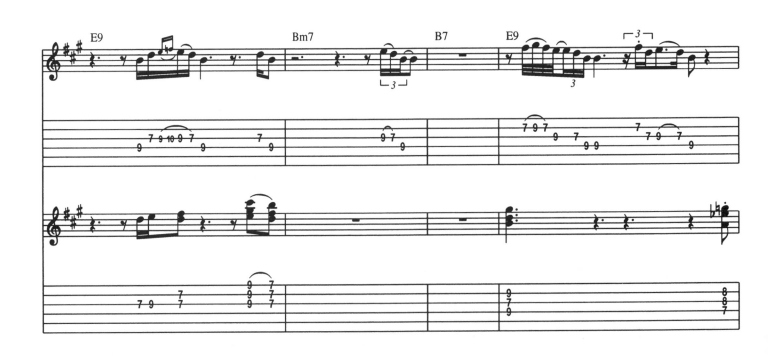

Gtr. 1: w/ Fill 3, 3rd time

Gtr. 2: w/ Fill 12, 3rd time

Oh how I hate to be — a-lone. —
to tell my trou-ble to.

My ba-by gone and left me. Some-one tell me what more, what more can I do.
My broth-er's in I-raq, and I don't know, I don't know what to do.

let ring

* full   1/2

* one finger bends both the A and the F♮ simultaneously

Fill 2
Gtr. 2

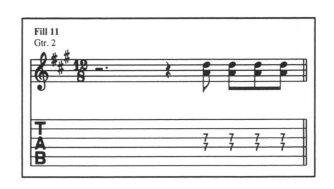

Fill 11
Gtr. 2

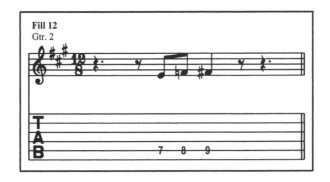

Fill 12
Gtr. 2

Gtr. 2: w/ Fill 13, 3rd time

Black night is fall - in'. _____ Oh how I hate to be ____ a - lone ___

Fill 3 ... **End Fill 3**

Gtr. 1: w/ Fill 5, 2nd time; w/ Fill 14, 3rd time
Gtr. 2: w/ Fill 4, 2nd time; w/ Fill 11, 3rd time
Gtr. 2: w/ Fill 4, 2nd time
Gtr. 2: w/ Fill 1, 1st time; tacet, 2nd time

I keep cry-in' for my ba-by.

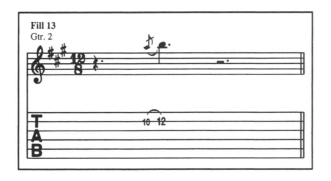

Fill 13
Gtr. 2

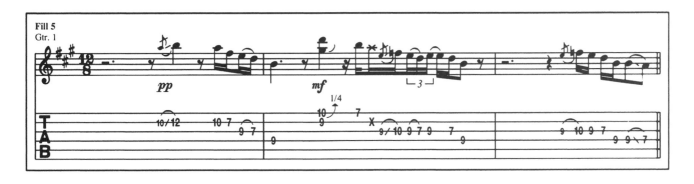

Fill 5
Gtr. 1

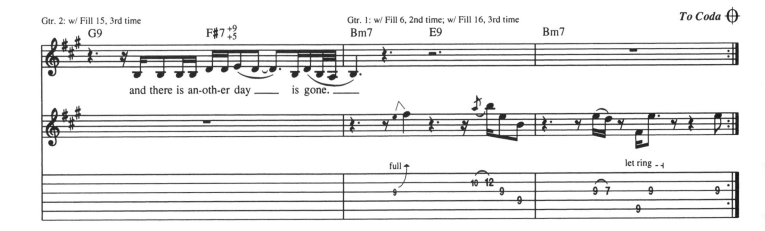

and there is an-oth-er day ____ is gone. ____

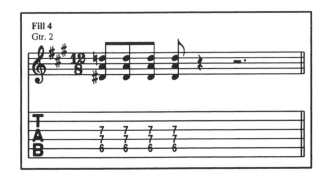

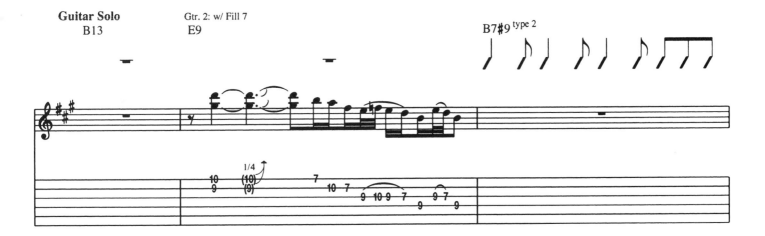

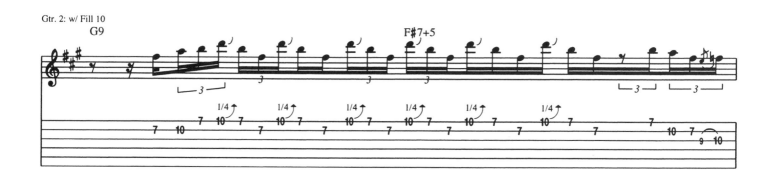

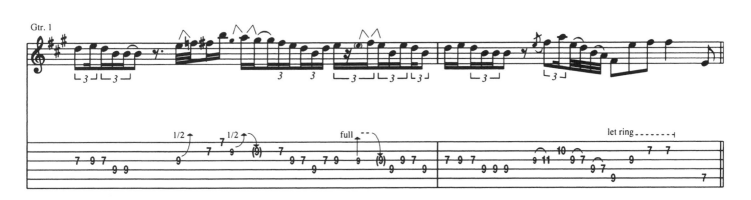

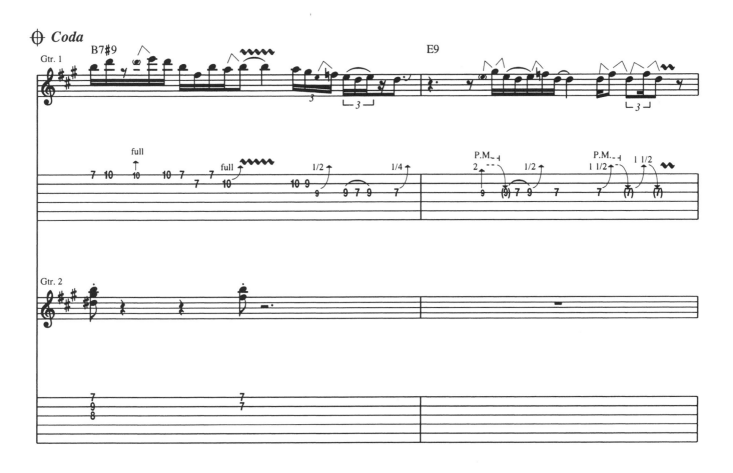

77

* bend is executed by pulling the string, not pushing

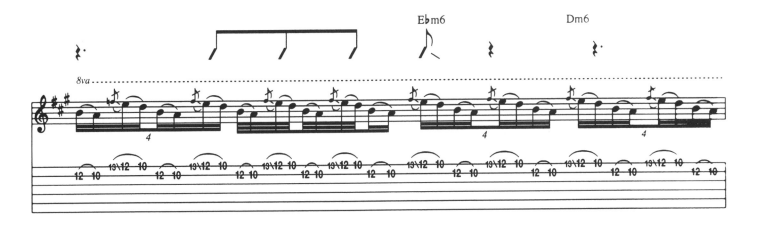

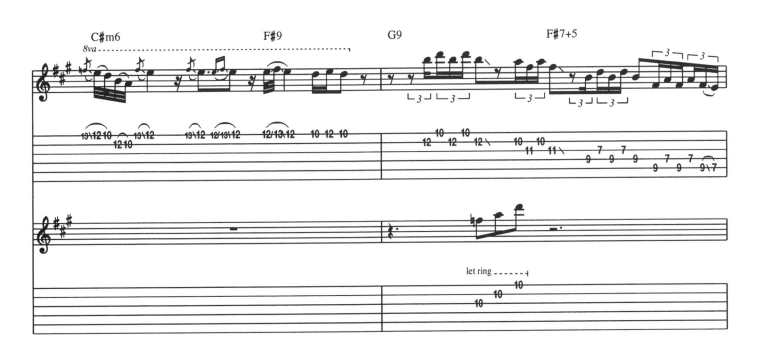

Let Me Love You Baby

Words and Music by Willie Dixon

* gradually release bend

ooh   whee   ba-by, you know a   Claire, _ you   sure look fine. _____

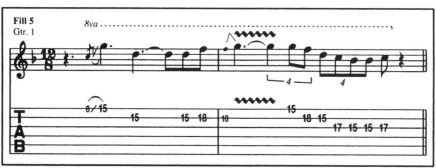

Fill 5
Gtr. 1

Fill 6
Gtr. 1

Fill 2
Gtr. 1

84

Gtr. 2: w/ Rhy. Fig. 1

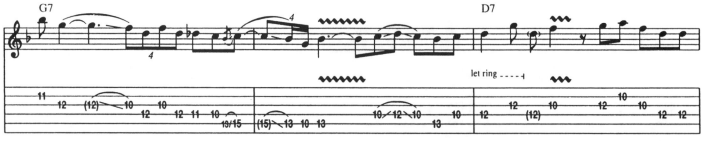

Additional Lyrics

Verse 2

Baby, when you walk you know you shake like a willow tree.
I say, baby, when you walk, woman, you know you shake like a willow tree.
Why does a girl like you love to make a fool of me.

Verses 3 & 5

Let me love you baby. Let me love you baby.
Let me love you baby. Let me love you baby.
Let me love you baby 'til your good love drive me crazy.

Verse 4

Well now baby, when you walk you know you shake like a willow tree.
Yah baby, when you walk, woman, you know you shake just like a willow tree.
Babe, a woman like you, ah would love to make a fool of me.

Rememberin' Stevie

By Buddy Guy

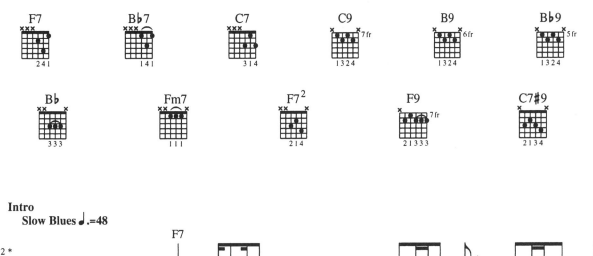

* Gtr. 2 is an approximate combination of the 2 rhythm gtr. parts

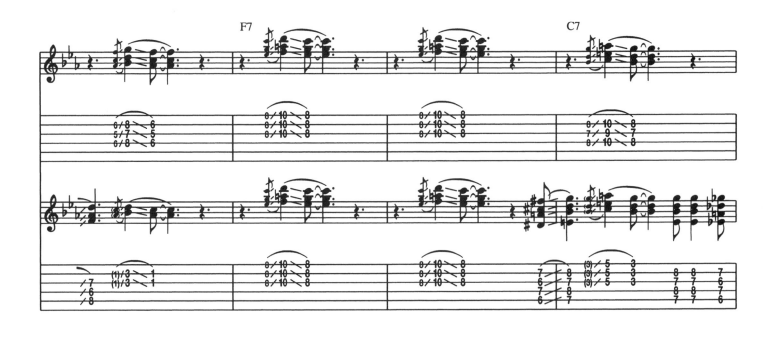

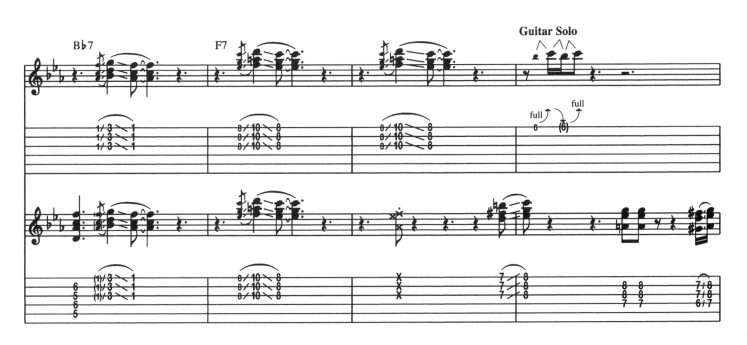

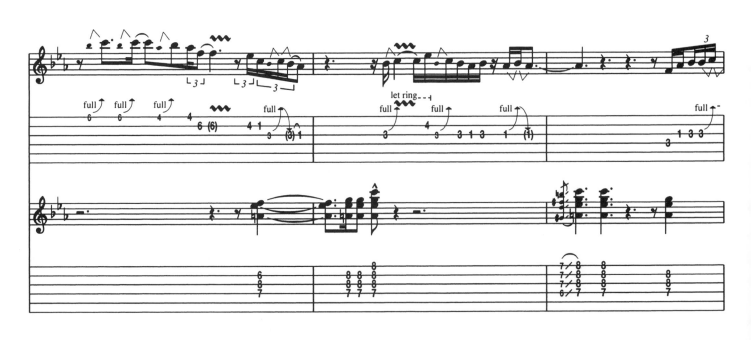

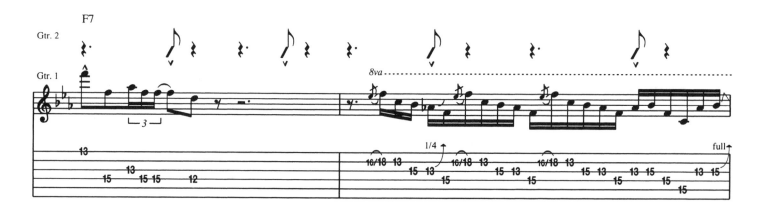

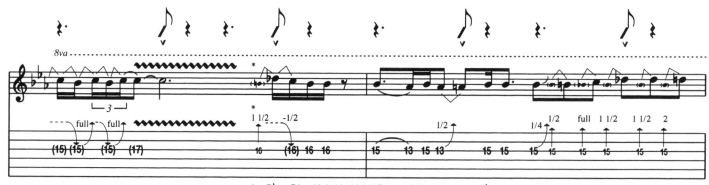

* as Bb to C bend is held with 3rd finger, 4th finger plays the Db and releases

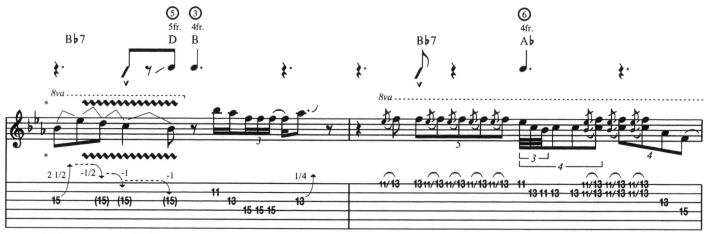

* vibrato occurs at top of 2nd note

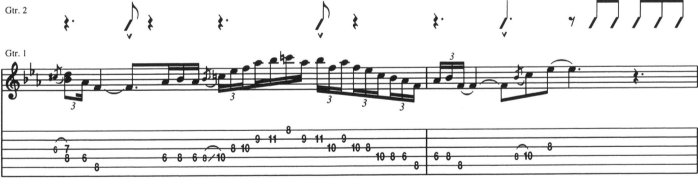

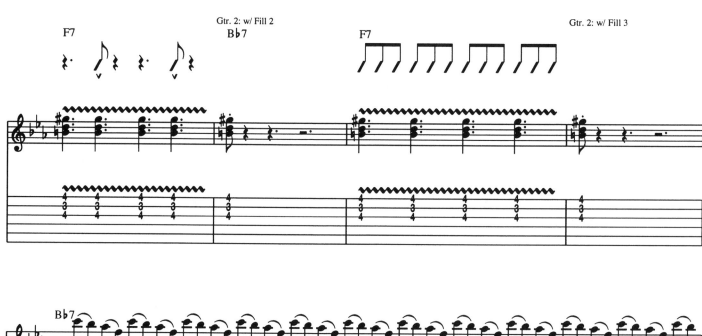

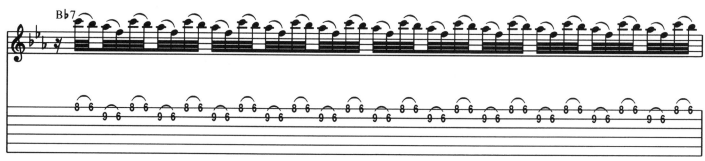

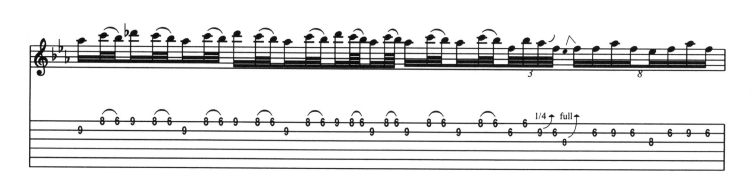

* Bb is bent 1/2 step, picked twice then picked again at full bend.

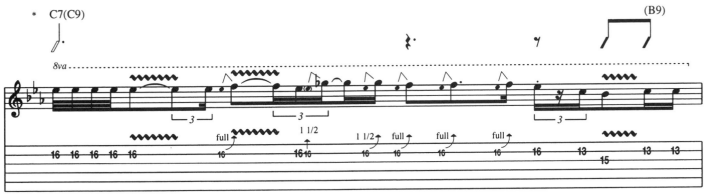

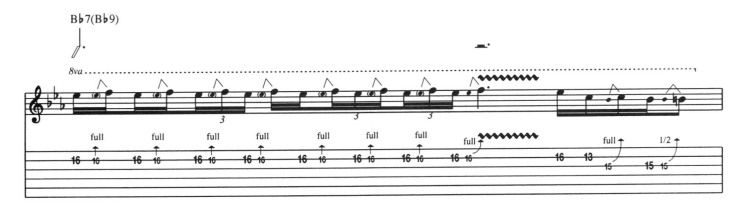

* chords in parenthesis are for slash notation

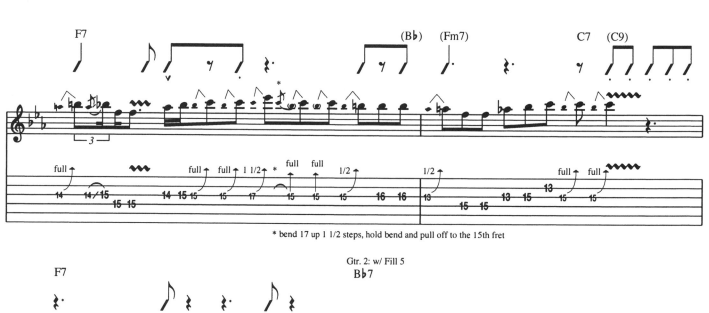

* bend 17 up 1 1/2 steps, hold bend and pull off to the 15th fret

Gtr. 2: w/ Fill 5

* fingerpicked

Gtr. 2: w/ Fill 6

Fill 5
Gtr. 2

Fill 6
Gtr. 2

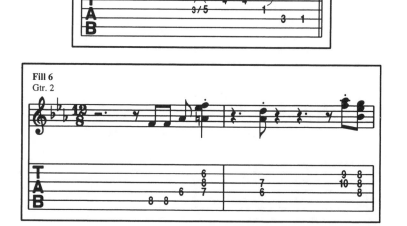

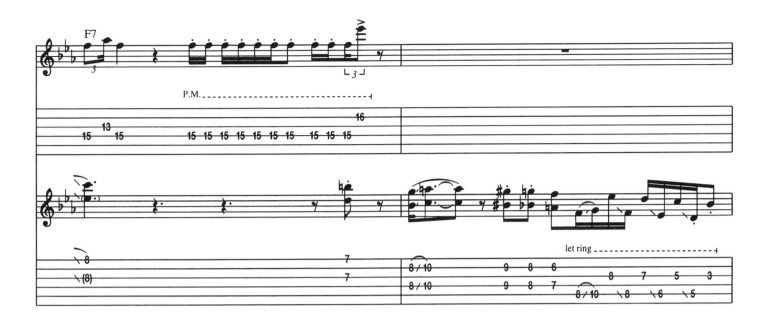

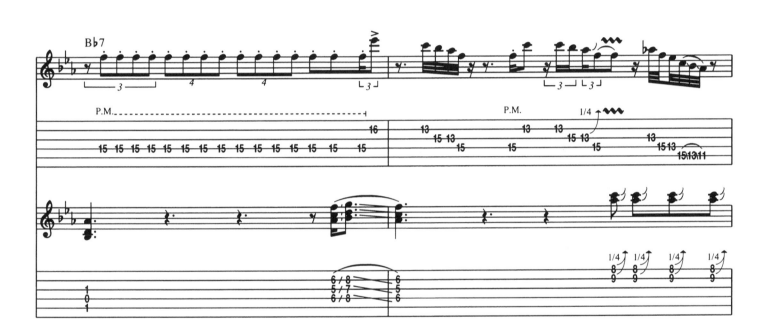

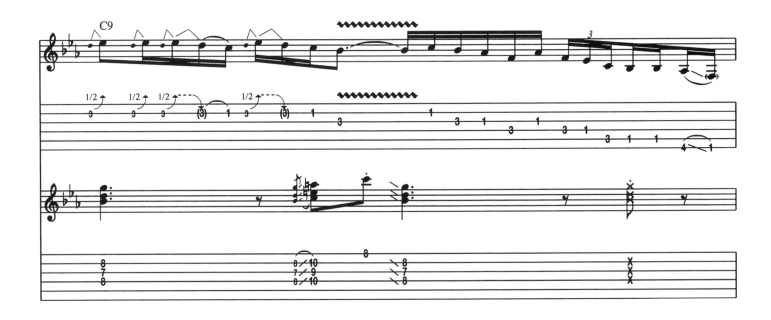

Guitar Notation Legend

Guitar Music can be notated three different ways: on a *musical staff*, in *tablature*, and in *rhythm slashes*.

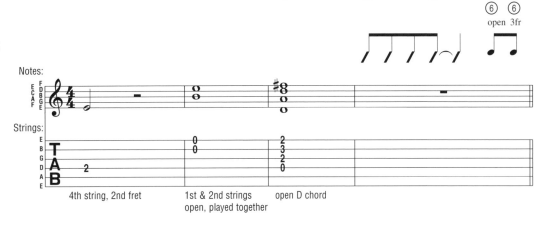

RHYTHM SLASHES are written above the staff. Strum chords in the rhythm indicated. Use the chord diagrams found at the top of the first page of the transcription for the appropriate chord voicings. Round noteheads indicate single notes.

THE MUSICAL STAFF shows pitches and rhythms and is divided by bar lines into measures. Pitches are named after the first seven letters of the alphabet.

TABLATURE graphically represents the guitar fingerboard. Each horizontal line represents a a string, and each number represents a fret.

4th string, 2nd fret

1st & 2nd strings open, played together

open D chord

Definitions for Special Guitar Notation

HALF-STEP BEND: Strike the note and bend up 1/2 step.

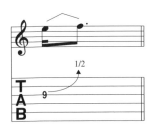

WHOLE-STEP BEND: Strike the note and bend up one step.

GRACE NOTE BEND: Strike the note and bend up as indicated. The first note does not take up any time.

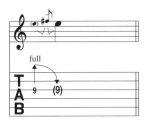

SLIGHT (MICROTONE) BEND: Strike the note and bend up 1/4 step.

BEND AND RELEASE: Strike the note and bend up as indicated, then release back to the original note. Only the first note is struck.

PRE-BEND: Bend the note as indicated, then strike it.

PRE-BEND AND RELEASE: Bend the note as indicated. Strike it and release the bend back to the original note.

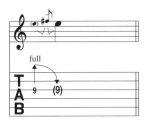

UNISON BEND: Strike the two notes simultaneously and bend the lower note up to the pitch of the higher.

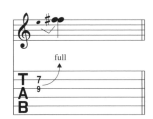

VIBRATO: The string is vibrated by rapidly bending and releasing the note with the fretting hand.

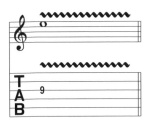

WIDE VIBRATO: The pitch is varied to a greater degree by vibrating with the fretting hand.

HAMMER-ON: Strike the first (lower) note with one finger, then sound the higher note (on the same string) with another finger by fretting it without picking.

PULL-OFF: Place both fingers on the notes to be sounded. Strike the first note and without picking, pull the finger off to sound the second (lower) note.

LEGATO SLIDE: Strike the first note and then slide the same fret-hand finger up or down to the second note. The second note is not struck.

SHIFT SLIDE: Same as legato slide, except the second note is struck.

TRILL: Very rapidly alternate between the notes indicated by continuously hammering on and pulling off.

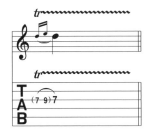

TAPPING: Hammer ("tap") the fret indicated with the pick-hand index or middle finger and pull off to the note fretted by the fret hand.

NATURAL HARMONIC: Strike the note while the fret-hand lightly touches the string directly over the fret indicated.

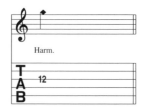

Harm.

PINCH HARMONIC: The note is fretted normally and a harmonic is produced by adding the edge of the thumb or the tip of the index finger of the pick hand to the normal pick attack.

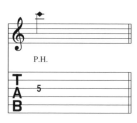

P.H.

HARP HARMONIC: The note is fretted normally and a harmonic is produced by gently resting the pick hand's index finger directly above the indicated fret (in parentheses) while the pick hand's thumb or pick assists by plucking the appropriate string.

H H

PICK SCRAPE: The edge of the pick is rubbed down (or up) the string, producing a scratchy sound.

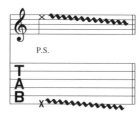

P.S.

MUFFLED STRINGS: A percussive sound is produced by laying the fret hand across the string(s) without depressing, and striking them with the pick hand.

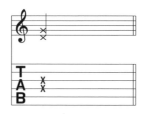

PALM MUTING: The note is partially muted by the pick hand lightly touching the string(s) just before the bridge.

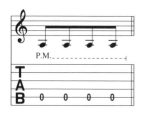

P.M.

RAKE: Drag the pick across the strings indicated with a single motion.

rake

TREMOLO PICKING: The note is picked as rapidly and continuously as possible.

ARPEGGIATE: Play the notes of the chord indicated by quickly rolling them from bottom to top.

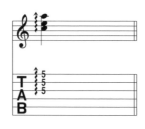

VIBRATO BAR DIVE AND RETURN: The pitch of the note or chord is dropped a specified number of steps (in rhythm) then returned to the original pitch.

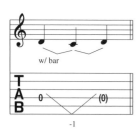

w/ bar

VIBRATO BAR SCOOP: Depress the bar just before striking the note, then quickly release the bar.

w/ bar

VIBRATO BAR DIP: Strike the note and then immediately drop a specified number of steps, then release back to the original pitch.

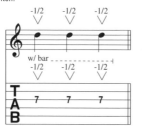

w/ bar

Additional Musical Definitions

 (accent)
- Accentuate note (play it louder)

 (accent)
- Accentuate note with great intensity

 (staccato)
- Play the note short

⊓
- Downstroke

V
- Upstroke

D.S. al Coda
- Go back to the sign (𝄋), then play until the measure marked "**To Coda**," then skip to the section labelled "**Coda**."

D.S. al Fine
- Go back to the beginning of the song and play until the measure marked "**Fine**" (end).

Rhy. Fig.
- Label used to recall a recurring accompaniment pattern (usually chordal).

Riff
- Label used to recall composed, melodic lines (usually single notes) which recur.

Fill
- Label used to identify a brief melodic figure which is to be inserted into the arrangement.

Rhy. Fill
- A chordal version of a Fill.

tacet
- Instrument is silent (drops out).

- Repeat measures between signs.

- When a repeated section has different endings, play the first ending only the first time and the second ending only the second time.

NOTE: Tablature numbers in parentheses mean:
1. The note is being sustained over a system (note in standard notation is tied), or
2. The note is sustained, but a new articulation (such as a hammer-on, pull-off, slide or vibrato begins, or
3. The note is a barely audible "ghost" note (note in standard notation is also in parentheses).